Strengthen Your Heart

Verses of Bitachon Attributed to the Maharal

How to Attain Supernatural Powers through the Torah

Based on פרקי מחשבה of Rav Yaakov Addes Slit''a

בס"ד

"MIKDASH"

KABALISTIC JEWISH MEDITATION "WAYS OF PEACE"

מיקד"ש – מדיטציה יהודית קבלית "דרכי שלום"

Written by: Rabbi Yakov Shepherd
Commentaries by: Yonatan Pason
Edited by: Ayalah Shepherd
Type setting and grafics by: Ayalah Shepherd

ISBN:
Softcover: 978-965-7025-71-0
Hardcover: 978-965-7025-72-7

Distributed by:
"Yeshivas Hamekubalim Nefesh HaChaim"
Israeli Non Profit Organization 580628527
For dedications, comments, & classes on
Kabbalistic meditations and much more

Please contact us at:
KingDavidKabbalah.com

From The Tomb of King David, Mount Zion - Jerusalem

לעילוי נשמת:

דניאל בן פלורה ולורי ז״ל

ולהבדיל בין החיים והמתים,

יהונתן לורי בן שרה (דמתקרייא סמדרה) שליט״א
להצלחה בגשמיות וברוחניות, לבנים זכרים
לעבודתו יתברך, ויזכה לכוחות הגוף והנפש מעל
הטבע, לקום מוקדם בכל לילה לעבודת ה'.

ומרים בת רחל תחי'

אלה שרה בת מרים תחי'

אמיליה רחל בת מרים תחי'
לבריאות, נחת ושמחה

שרה (דמתקרייא סמדרה) **בת רוזה** תחי'

יעל פלורה בת שרה (דמתקרייא סמדרה) תחי'

רוזה בת בוקה ג'ודיה תחי'
שיזכו לחזור בתשובה שלמה.

הרב אשר בן נחמה שליט״א

הרבנית רחל בת פלה פייגה תחי'
לבריאות נחת ואריכות ימים

ישיבת התפוצות תורת ישראל ע.ר. 580016509
DIASPORA YESHIVA TORAS YISRAEL

הר ציון, ת.ד. 6426, ירושלים 91063
טל': 02-6716841, פקס: 02-6729493, דוא"ל: Reservation.d.y@gmail.com
אתר: mountzioninfo.com , www.diasporayeshiva.com
Mount Zion, P.O.B. 6426, Zip Code 91063 Jerusalem, Israel
Rabbi Dr. Mordecai Goldstein, Dean and Rosh Yeshiva
בנשיאות הרה"ג מרדכי גולדשטיין שליט"א ראש הישיבה

נברך לא-לקינו שבראנו לכבודו ונתן לנו תורת אמת- הכלולה מפשט, רמז, דרש, וסוד.

וחיי עולם נתן בתוכינו- עבודת הלב היא התפילה, גם היא כלולה מכל החלקים הנ"ל. וכבר אמרו חכמים ז"ע על התפילה שהיא הסולם המוצב ארצה וראשו מגיע השמימה.

ועוד אמרו ז"ל, שלא יעשה תפילתו קבע, אלא תחנונים וכמה צריכים אנו להודות להלל ולשבח, שזכינו ויצא מישבתינו פרי נאה זה- סידור בנוסח אשכנז עם כוונות האר"י ז"ל. חידוש נפלא שלא היה כמותו עד היום, והוא קילורין לעיניים ומתק שפתיים, וניםוקו בצידו, הסברים נאים ומתוקנים על עיקרי הכוונות, אשר כתב תלמידי כבני, הרב הגאון ר' יעקב אברהם שפהרד שליט"א, אשר לומד ומלמד בישיבתינו זה שנים רבות, וכבר סמכתי ידי עליו ל"יורה יורה ידין ידין", ועוד דחק עצמו וזכה ונכנס לעולם מעין עולם הבא- חכמת הקבלה. ולמד אצל חכמים גדולים ומפורסמים, בדרך ישראל סבא, בספר הזהר הקדוש, כתבי האר"י ז"ל והרב הרש"ש. זכה וקטף מעץ החיים, וגם הביאו לנו לטעום ולהתענג מזיו השכינה, כי בא מועד.

ולאחר שראיתי כן, הורואתי לו שיפתח ישיבה מיוחדת ללימוד החכמה הזו, מתחת לקבר דוד המע"ה, וקראנו לישיבה 'נפש החיים' – על שם חיבורו המפורסם של הגאון המקובל ר' חיים מוולוז'ין – גדול תלמידי הגר"א, להורות כי דרכינו בקודש, מושתת על היסודות האיתנים שאותם הציב בספרו.

עוד צריך להוסיף ולאמר כי סידור קדוש זה נכתב בדיבוק חברים ופלפול התלמידים, כולם אנשי קומה בלימוד הקדוש הזה וכן בכל חלקי התורה, ועבר ניפוי אחר ניפוי שיהיה ראוי לצאת לאור עולם ב"ה.

אשרינו מה טוב חלקינו ומה נעים גורלנו, ואשרי כל מי שיתפלל בזה הסידור, להרבות כבוד שמיים וכבוד התורה, להחיש גאולתנו, שתגיע במהרה בימינו, ונראה בבנין בית מקדשינו ומשיח צדקינו, אמן סלה.

בברכת התורה ולומדיה

הרב מרדכי גולדשטיין

ראש הישיבה

<table>
<tr><td>

Rabbi Avraham Goldstien

Ram Diaspora Yeshiva Toras Yisrael

Moreh Horaha of Mount Zion and Old City

</td><td>

אברהם גולדשטיין

ר"מ ישיבת התפוצות תורת ישראל

ומו"צ הר ציון והעיר העתיקה

</td></tr>
</table>

I am pleased to offer my wholehearted recommendation for "Strenthen Your Heart", a compilation of verces from the Tanach, featuring insightful commentaries and kabbalistic guidance by Rabbi Yakov Shepherd.

I have had the privilege of witnessing Rabbi Shepherd's unwavering dedication to helping individuals draw closer to Hashem through the deep wisdom of Kabbalistic meditation and learning. His work reflects a rare combination of spiritual depth, clarity, and compassion.

Over the years, I have enthusiastically recommended several of Rabbi Shepherd's publications, including "The Kabbalistic Meditations", which stands out as a true gem among his many contributions. "Strengthen Your Heart" is no exception. It offers readers not only a window into Rabbi Shepherd's knowledge, but also a practical path toward a life of inner calm, trust (bitachon), and faith (emunah).

Rabbi Shepherd's insights and heartfelt guidance have the potential to make a meaningful and lasting impact on those who engage with his teachings.

It is with great enthusiasm that I extend my humble blessings to all those who embrace ""Strenthen Your Heart" as well as his other publications and teachings as a means to deepen their connection with Hashem. May they find tremendous success along their paths and experience abundant happiness within their homes.

May this book bring enlightenment, joy, and fulfillment to all who use it.

With the Blessings of the Torah,

בס"ד

הרבנות והמועצה הדתית
באר-שבע

Rabbi YEHUDA DERY
Chief Rabbi and Head of Rabbinical Courts
Beer-Sheva, ISRAEL.
חודש 'ליהודים היתה אורה'
אדר התשע"ז

הרב יהודה דרעי
הרב הראשי וראש אבות בתי הדין
באר-שבע

אגרת ברכה

הנני בזה להוקיר ולהכיר לאחרים את מעלת הרה"ג רבי יעקב אברהם שפהרד שליט"א ראש בית המדרש ליודעי ח"ן בקבר דוד המלך ע"ה – הר ציון עיה"ק ירושלים תובב"א.

ביודעי ומכירי קאמינא עוד מתקופת לימודיו בישיבת התפוצות בחבורת לומדי ההלכה בארבעת חלקי שו"ע, והשתתף במשך כמה שנים בשיעורים הקבועים שמסרתי בפני בני החבורה, וגם נבחן בהצלחה בכל המבחנים שערכנו תמידין כסדרן. בשנים אלו שקד על תלמודו והיה לאחד מבחירי החבורה הן בחכמתו והן ביראתו הקודמת לחכמתו.

והנה בשנים האחרונות חשקה נפשו בלימוד תורת הח"ן וגם זכה להקים חבורא קדישא על ציון קבר דוד המלך ע"ה ובהם הוא שוקד על תלמודו יומם ולילה ומתחסד עם קונו בנקיות ויראת ה' טהורה, וגם זכה כבר לחבר כמה חיבורים והוציאם לאור עולם. והן זה היום שמחתי לשמוע כי הולך להדפיס סידור ח"ן.

והנני לברכו כי חפץ ה' בידו יצלח להגדיל תורה ולהאדירה ברוב נחת דקדושא לאורך ימים ושנות חיים, אמן.

הכ"ח לכבוד התורה ולומדיה

יהודה דרעי
הרב הראשי וראב"ד באר שבע

לשכת הרבנות: רחוב התלמוד 8, באר-שבע, טל: 08-6204007, פקס. 08-6651204

ב"ה י"ז לחודש אדר ב' תשע"ו

מכתב ברכה

שמחתי בראותי את מלאכת הקודש של ידידי הרב יעקב אברהם שפרד שליט"א
ראש ישיבת "נפש החיים" על יד קבר דוד המלך ללימוד תורת הח"ן, שהוא ת"ח
ועוסק בתורה לשמה מתוך הדחק, וכעת רחש לבו להוציא לאור סידור נוסח
אשכנז עם כוונות שמיוסדים עפ"י האריז"ל והרש"ש. והגם שאין לנו עסק
כמכוונים, עכ"ז אמינא לפעלא טבא לאוקמי שכינתא מעפרא, על ידי העסק
בתורת הקבלה שבזה תלויה הגאולה השלימה בב"א, ושיזכה להגדיל תורה
ולהאדירה מתוך בריות גופא ונהורא מעליא.

בברכת התורה

משה חיים בלאאמו"ר אברהם זצ"ל

ברנדוויין

בס"ד   כ"ח מנחם אב תשע"ט

ברכה והסכמה

שמחתי בראותי כי תלמידי הגדול, **הרב יעקב אברהם שפהרד שליט"א,**
מרביץ תורה בכל הפרד"ס בקבר דוד המלך, הולך מחיל אל חיל ומוציא לאור בכל
שנה כמעט ספרים וסידורים חדשים, ואברכו כי חפץ ה' בידו יצליח, ויזכה לקדש ה'
בכל מעשיו.

ויש להוסיף, כי הרב שפהרד, ישב לצידי בשיעורים בתורת הרש"ש הקדוש במשך
עשר שנים, וראיתי כי אכן בעל הבנה עמוקה הוא, וראוי הוא ללמוד וללמד את
תורת הקבלה לעם ישראל אשר בכל אתר ואתר, ואף אני מפנה אליו תלמידים
המגיעים אלי, בעיקר דוברי אנגלית, הצריכים את עזרתו שיתרגם ויבאר להם את
דברי האר"י ז"ל והרש"ש זיע"א.

אשרי חלקם של הרב שפהרד, תלמידיו וכל המסייעים בהפצת חכמת הקבלה אשר
למד ולימד כאן בעיר העתיקה של ירושלים תובב"א, לכל העולם בכמה שפות, כי
אכן עת לעשות לה', ויש להביא לעם ישראל שבכל התפוצות הקדמות אמיתיות
לעורר בהם הלבבות, ולהקיץ נרדמים, בתקווה שנזכה כולנו לראות בשיבת ציון
ובניין בית המקדש בקרוב ממש.

כה לחי
ובברכת התורה ולומדיה
הרב ישראל אביחי שליט"א
ראש ישיבת המקובלים
"בית אל"
שבין החומות
עיה"ק ירושלים תובב"א

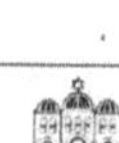

ישיבת "בית אל" רחוב בית אל 9 ירושלים 9751650
ת. ד. 14123 ירושלים מיקוד: 9114101
Fax: 02/626-3413 פקס - Phone: 02/627-5073 טלפון

The Holy Kabalistic "Beit-El" Yeshiva
9 Beit-El Street Jerusalem 9751650
P. O. Box 14123 Old City Jerusalem ISRAEL

HaRav Avigdor Nebenzahl

הרב אביגדר יחזקאל נבנצל

רב בירושלים העתיקה תובב"א
מח"ס ביצחק יקרא
מציון מכלל יופי
שיחות לחמישה חומשי תורה ומועדים

בס"ד, תאריך ___

כאשר הרב הגאון ר' יעקב אברהם שפהרד שליט"א, ראש ישיבת נפש החיים, מפארי עדת הקודש, פה עיר הקודש תובב"א, מו"ל ספרים המיוסדים על תורת הקבלה, רבותינו מצוקי ארץ זי"ע, ואמנם אין דרכי לבא בהסכמות על דברים העוסקים בזה, לא נצרכה אלא לברכה, כי הנ"ל תלמיד חכם העוסק בתורת ה' ימים ולילות בחכמה, ומעמיד תלמידים יראי שמים. ועל כן, ידי תכון עמו לברכו שיפוצו מעיינותיו חוצה וישב על התורה ועבודת ה', מתוך שמחה והרחבה, ולהפקד לכתיבה וחתימה טובה עם כל ישראל ושמחת עולם על ראשם בביאת משיח

בברכת כתיבה וחתימה טובה

צעיר הלוי

אביגדר נבנצל

בס"ד

ישיבת התפוצות תורת ישראל ע.ר. 580016509
DIASPORA YESHIVA TORAS YISRAEL
הר ציון, ת.ד. 6426, ירושלים 91063
טל' משרד: 02-6716841, 02-6232969 פקס: 02-6729493
Reservation.d.y@gmail.com, 6716841@gmail.com, www.diasporayeshiva.com

Recommendation for "Strenthen Your Heart", book of Emunah and Bitachon.

The author of Siddur Zichron David, Sidur Chen, Sidur Hayare and Kabbalistic Meditations for the Nations and more is now publishing a strenthening new book. It is my hope that more books are translated from Hebrew to English Spanish, French and other languages that introduce Kabbalah ideas, such as Kavannot and Jewish Mediation to beginners. The author, my student, the Mekubal Rav HaGaon Rabbi Yaakov Avraham Shepherd, Rosh Yeshiva of Yeshivat Nefesh Ha'Chaim, on Mt. Zion, has already proved himself in publishing siddurs and other various books for Advanced students and also beginners to benefit Talmidei Chachamim involved in Kabbalah.

There is no doubt that there is a critical need and "et laasot l'Hashem" since there are already many ignorant people empty from Torah and Mitzvot that are printing wrong translations of the Wisdom of the Kabbalah and causing great damage. Therefore, this valuable contribution of publishing a correct translation with yirat shamayim the Rabbi will fix the damage that was caused by previous books.

I heard that my father the HaGaon Rav Dr Mordechai Goldstein "told Rabbi Shepherd to work on translating and publishing books on Kabbalah. It is not only the right thing to do but also the right time to do it." After seeing the draft of the Book, I support and encourage this project and give my blessings to all the people that are involved in helping this important work.

May all of those who supported and worked and use this book and others that he publishes see great pleasure and joy for what they have accomplished. May they merit seeing the Final Redemption and rebuilding of the Beit HaMikdash.

With Torah Blessings,

בברכת התורה ולומדיה
יצחק בן לאמו"ר הכ"מ הרה"ג מורדכי גולדשטיין
ראש ישיבת "התפוצות", "תורת ישראל", רבה של הר ציון.

Strengthen Your Heart

Verces of Bitachon Attributed to the Maharal

Introduction

A Renewed Gateway to Bitachon

This work presents a newly refined and spiritually illuminated edition of the classic verses on bitachon (trust in Hashem), attributed to the Maharal of Prague. Following the traditional alef-bet structure, these verses are arranged in a meaningful spiritual sequence — one that guides the reader toward deeper emunah and menuchat hanefesh.

Each verse is carefully laid out in four components:

- The original Hebrew text
- A literal English translation
- A phonetic transliteration
- A spiritual explanation, enriched with insights from Chassidus, Kabbalah, and classic Mussar

What Makes This Edition Unique

This is more than a translation. It is a new commentary and spiritual guide, designed to be both usable and up lifting.

- Verses are atributed to the Maharal of Prague.
- Accessible: Designed for English speakers who may or may not be fluent in Hebrew.
- Elevated: Each verse is illuminated with explanations drawn from the teachings of the Maharal, the Zohar, the Tanya, Orchos Tzaddikim, Sfas Emes, the Baal Shem Tov, the Ramchal, and others.
- This is a tool not just for study — but for daily meditation, spiritual clarity, and connection to Hashem in all areas of life

The Inner Meaning of Bitachon

Rabbeinu HaGaon HaRav Yitzchak Zev Soloveitchik (the Brisker Rav) explained the verse in Tehillim (27:14):
"Hope to Hashem, strengthen yourself, and He will give courage to your heart — and hope to Hashem."

This means: the great reward for one who trusts in Hashem is that Hashem strengthens his heart and gives him the power to trust even more. In return for one's bitachon, he is given Divine help to deepen and expand his trust — creating a higher and higher inner foundation of security and joy.

So too writes Rabbeinu Bachya in Chovot HaLevavot:
A man may possess wealth, property, and power — yet live in fear and anxiety, always threatened by loss or enemies. But the one who has bitachon in Hashem removes worry from his heart, lives with calm, and lacks for nothing. His joy is rooted in knowing that all he needs, Hashem will provide.

This is the deeper meaning of the verse:
"Kaveh el Hashem… ve-kaveh el Hashem" trust brings more trust. That is the ultimate reward.

Livelihood and the Divine Decree

Chazal taught (Beitzah 16a):
"A person's sustenance is decreed on Rosh Hashanah."

Why does it say sustenance (mezonotav) and not money (kesef)?
Because Hashem decrees how much actual food and sustenance — not currency — a person will receive: bread, milk, eggs, coffee, everything for his needs.

Even if inflation rises, or the economy crashes, one who trusts in Hashem is not shaken. He knows that Hashem accounted for all of it — in advance. He joyfully recites every morning:
"Wealth and honor come from You, and You rule over all" (Divrei HaYamim I 29:12).

As it says in Midrash Rabbah (Behar 34:11): **"The bread is already sliced"** — meaning the decree has already been issued, and no one can alter it.

Insights from Orchos Tzaddikim
The Gate of Joy

(Adapted and translated)
The sage said: Every person needs a boundary, a support, a foundation to uphold his good deeds.

What is that foundation?

Bitachon — trust in Hashem. As it says:

"Cast your burden upon Hashem, and He will sustain you" (Tehillim 55:23).

What gives birth to bitachon?

Emunah — faith. One who believes that all success in this world and the next comes only from Hashem will naturally come to love Him with all his heart.

And what creates true emunah?

Acceptance of adversity with joy.

Just like a loyal servant who knows his master is generous and kind, and pays his workers well — such a servant works happily, even when the labor is difficult, knowing the reward is great. But if the master is stingy, the servant serves reluctantly.

So too, one who truly believes in Hashem — that He is good, merciful, and just — will accept life's trials with inner joy. He knows that every hardship is repaid with eternal sweetness.

As Chazal said:
Nebuchadnezzar merited kingship for walking a few steps in Hashem's honor.

Eisav merited worldly success for honoring his father.

If so, how much more must we rejoice in doing Hashem's will — knowing that He exchanges mere copper coins for golden crowns.

Seven Foundations of Bitachon

(from Orchos Tzaddikim, paraphrased and condensed)

1. Hashem loves you more than anyone and watches over you constantly.

2. Every good thing that comes to you from others is from Hashem alone.

3. Hashem gives from kindness, not because you earned it.

4. No one can alter His decree — not to add, not to take away.

5. He knows your inner truth — trust must be genuine.

6. To trust Him, you must serve Him — if you ignore His commands, your bitachon is false.

7. Your effort is part of His plan — but success does not come from your job or your tools. All comes from Him, and He has infinite ways to provide.

A person should view all human help like a chain of blind people — each one guided by another, but all ultimately led by the one seeing man at the front. That "seer" is Hashem. All help we receive from others is simply a tool in His hand.

We are all blind without Him.

This sefer was created as a living guide — to help every soul learn to trust, to internalize Emunah and bitachon, and to grow into the spiritual freedom that comes with it.

It is not a collection of verses. It is a path to inner liberation

Aleph

Trust in Hashem

אַשְׁרֵי הַגֶּבֶר אֲשֶׁר שָׂם יְהוָה מִבְטַחוֹ
וְלֹא פָנָה אֶל רְהָבִים וְשָׂטֵי כָזָב

Transliteration: Ashrei ha-gever asher sam Hashem mivtacho, ve-lo fanah el rehavim ve-shatei kazav; Tehillim 40:5

Translation: Praiseworthy is the man who places his trust in Hashem and does not turn to the arrogant or those who stray after falsehood.

Insight: The true bitachon involves fully placing oneself in Hashem's care and refusing to depend on worldly powers or manipulative means. The Chazon Ish (Emunah uVitachon ch. 2) adds that such trust must be exclusive — partial reliance is not true bitachon, and invites inner confusion.

Sources:
Rav Tzadok, Tzidkat HaTzaddik §198
Chazon Ish, Emunah uVitachon ch. 2

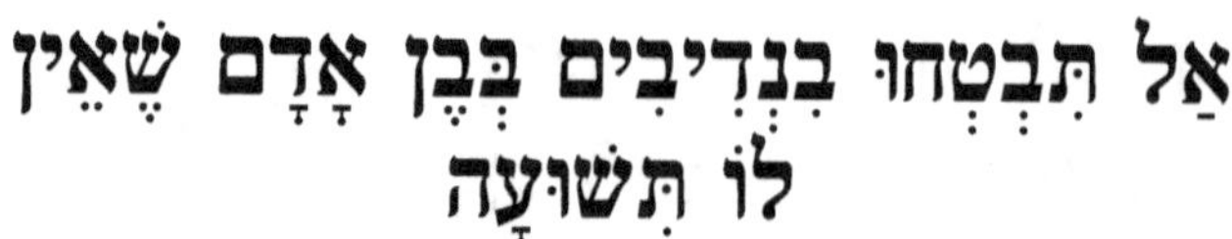

אַל תִּבְטְחוּ בִנְדִיבִים בְּבֶן אָדָם שֶׁאֵין
לוֹ תְּשׁוּעָה

Transliteration: Al tivtechu b'nedivim, b'ven adam she'ein lo teshuah; Tehillim 146:3

Translation: Do not trust in nobles, in a human being who has no salvation.

Insight: Chovot HaLevavot (Sha'ar HaBitachon ch. 1) writes that it is foolish to rely on any being that cannot even save itself. Real salvation comes only from Hashem, and attributing power to people is spiritual error.

Source:
Chovot HaLevavot, Sha'ar HaBitachon, ch. 1
Chazon Ish, Emunah uVitachon ch. 2

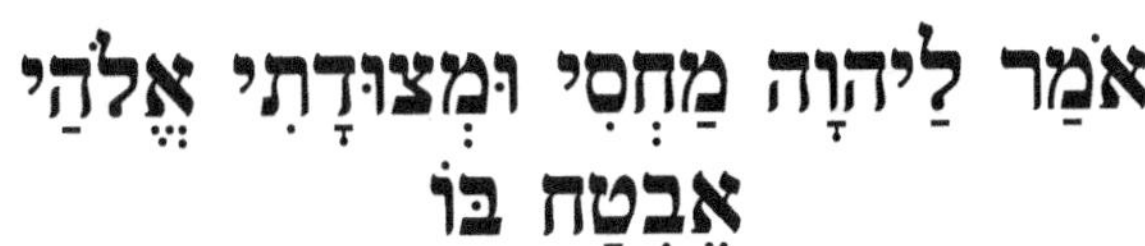

אֹמַר לַיהוָה מַחְסִי וּמְצוּדָתִי אֱלֹהַי אֶבְטַח בּוֹ

Transliteration: Omar la-Hashem machsi u-metzudati, Elohai evtach bo: Tehillim 91:2

Translation: I say to Hashem: "My refuge and my fortress, my God — I trust in Him."

Insight: Rebbe Nosson of Breslov explains (Likutey Halachot, Birkas HaMazon 5:12) that articulating trust in Hashem strengthens one's inner commitment. The verbal declaration "I trust in Him" activates awareness and draws divine protection.

Source:
Likutey Halachot, Birkas HaMazon 5:12

אֱלֹהַי בְּךָ בָטַחְתִּי אַל אֵבוֹשָׁה אַל יַעַלְצוּ אוֹיְבַי לִי

Transliteration: Elohai becha batachti, al evosha, al ya'altzu oyvai li; Tehillim 25:2

Translation: My God, in You I have trusted; let me not be shamed; let not my enemies rejoice over me.

Insight: The Chafetz Chaim (Shem Olam I ch. 7) emphasizes that true bitachon includes praying not to be publicly disgraced, so as not to weaken others' faith. Rashi explains that shame here means spiritual failure — that one's trust should be vindicated by divine response.

Sources:
Shem Olam, Part I, ch. 7
Rashi on Tehillim 25:2

Transliteration: Eilecha za'aku ve-nimlatu, vecha batchu ve-lo voshu Tehillim 22:6

Translation: To You they cried out and were rescued; in You they trusted and were not shamed.

Insight: Rabbeinu Yonah (Shaarei Teshuvah 3:32) teaches that recalling past salvations strengthens present trust. The Sefat Emet (Beshalach 5641) writes that memory of Hashem's kindness reawakens divine compassion in every generation.

Sources:
Shaarei Teshuvah 3:32
Sefat Emet, Beshalach 5641

אַל־תִּבְטְחוּ בְעֹשֶׁק וּבְגָזֵל אַל־תֶּהְבָּלוּ
חַיִל כִּי־יָנוּב אַל־תָּשִׁיתוּ לֵב

Transliteration: Al tivtechu be-oshek u-ve-gazel, al thabalu chayil; ki yinaveh, al tasimu lev Tehillim 62:11

Translation: Do not trust in oppression and have false hopes in robbery; if wealth increases, do not set your heart on it [ignore it].

Insight: Mesillat Yesharim (ch. 21) warns that trusting in wealth leads to arrogance and spiritual blindness. True trust resides not in possessions, but in Hashem who gives and takes. The righteous detach emotionally even when they work for a livelihood.

Source:
Mesillat Yesharim, ch. 21

אָז תֵּלֵךְ לָבֶטַח דַּרְכֶּךָ וְרַגְלְךָ לֹא תִגֹּף

Transliteration: Az telech la-vetach darkecha, ve-raglecha lo tigof ; Mishlei 3:23

Translation: Then you will walk securely on your path, and your foot will not stumble.

Insight: The Malbim explains that "secure walking" means being protected even from unforeseen obstacles. The Tanya (ch. 42) connects this to da'at — a deep, inner awareness of Hashem's presence that stabilizes one's path in life.

Sources:
Malbim on Mishlei 3:23
Tanya, ch. 42

אִם תַּחֲנֶה עָלַי מַחֲנֶה לֹא יִירָא לִבִּי אִם תָּקוּם עָלַי מִלְחָמָה בְּזֹאת אֲנִי בוֹטֵחַ

Transliteration: Im tachane alai machaneh, lo yira libi; im takum alai milchamah — b'zot ani boteach; Tehillim 27:3

Translation: If an army encamps against me, my heart will not fear; if war arises against me, in this I trust.

Insight: Reb Nosson of Breslov (Likutey Halachot, O.C. 4:13) says "in this" refers to Torah — the anchor of bitachon. The Midrash teaches that David's power in battle came not from weapons, but from his covenant with Hashem and trust in His word.

Source:
Likutey Halachot, O.C. 4:13 (Breslov)

Beit
Trust Rooted in Strength and Surrender

בָּרוּךְ הַגֶּבֶר אֲשֶׁר יִבְטַח בַּיהוָה וְהָיָה
יְהוָה מִבְטַחוֹ

Transliteration: Baruch ha-gever asher yivtach b'Hashem, ve-hayah Hashem mivtacho; Yirmiyahu 17:7

Translation: Blessed is the man who trusts in Hashem, and Hashem will be his security.

Insight: Rav Tzadok HaKohen (Tzidkat HaTzaddik §198) explains that when one's essence is given over entirely to Hashem, he becomes a vessel through which divine influence flows uninterruptedly. Trust becomes not only a mindset but an ongoing connection to blessings of abundance.

Source:
Tzidkat HaTzaddik §198

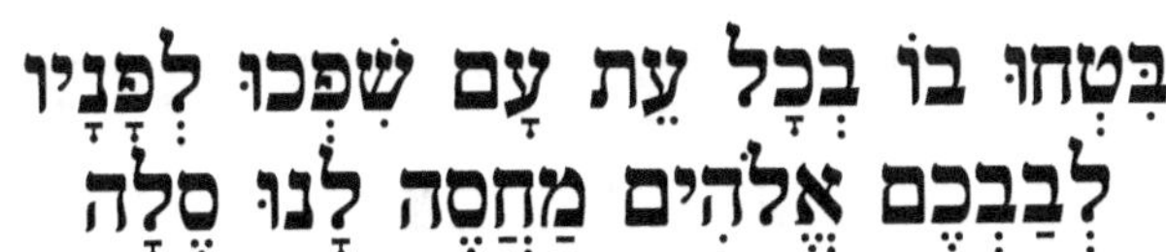

Transliteration: Bitchu vo b'chol et, am; shifchu lefanav levavchem — Elokim machaseh lanu, selah; Tehillim 62:9

Translation: Trust in Him at all times, O people; pour out your hearts before Him. Elokim is our refuge — forever.

Insight: The Orchos Tzaddikim (Sha'ar HaSimchah) teaches that bitachon brings emotional openness — when one trusts deeply, he no longer represses his heart. True simchah flows from heartfelt surrender to Hashem's will, especially in tefillah.

Source:
Orchos Tzaddikim, Sha'ar HaSimchah

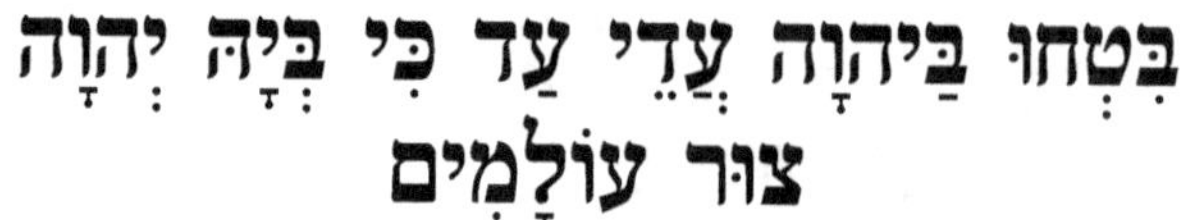

בִּטְחוּ בַיהוָה עֲדֵי עַד כִּי בְּיָה יְהוָה
צוּר עוֹלָמִים

Transliteration: Bitchu ba-Hashem adei ad, ki b'Yah Hashem Tzur olamim; Yeshayahu 26:4

Translation: Trust in Hashem forever, for in God (Yah), Hashem is the Rock of all worlds (eternity).

Insight: The Nefesh HaChaim (Sha'ar 3, ch. 12) explains that "Yah" represents the yichud (unification) of Chochmah and Binah — by trusting in Hashem's unity, one attaches to the eternal root of creation. It is the secret of resilience beyond time.

Source:
Nefesh HaChaim, Sha'ar 3, ch. 12

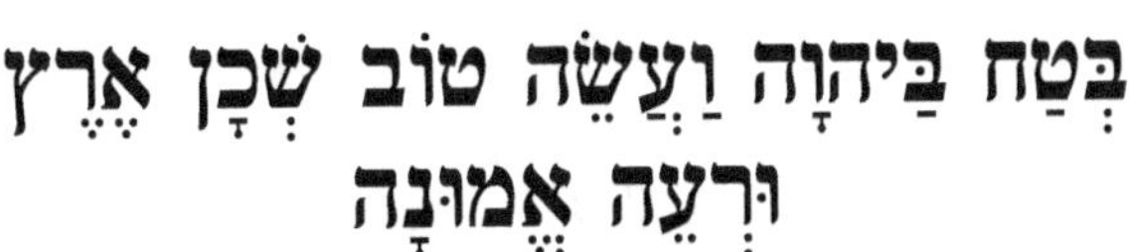

בְּטַח בַּיהוָה וַעֲשֵׂה טוֹב שְׁכָן אֶרֶץ
וּרְעֵה אֱמוּנָה

Transliteration: Betach ba-Hashem va'aseh tov; shechon eretz u're'eh emunah; Tehillim 37:3

Translation: Trust in Hashem and do good; dwell in the land and nurture faith.

Insight: The Sfas Emes (Vayeshev 5643) says that faith grows through consistent good deeds. Trust alone is the root, but "doing good" is the watering that gives life. Without practice, even strong bitachon may not take root in this world.

Source:
Sfas Emes, Vayeshev 5643

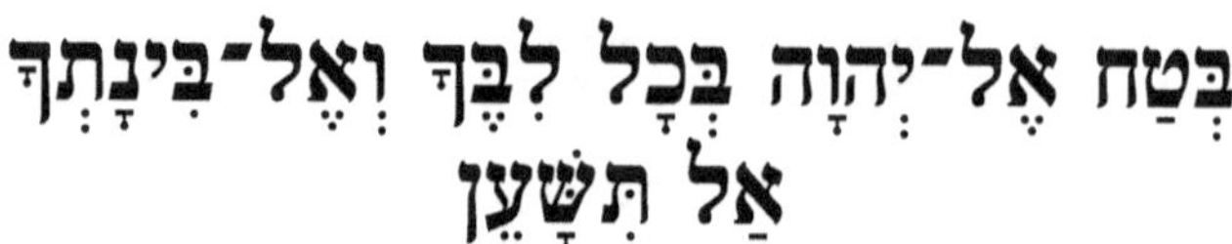

Transliteration: Betach el-Hashem b'chol libecha, ve'el binatcha al tisha'en; Mishlei 3:5

Translation: Trust in Hashem with all your heart, and do not rely on your own understanding.

Insight: Chovot HaLevavot (Sha'ar HaBitachon ch. 3) emphasizes that rational thought is limited only by surrendering intellect to the Divine can one receive clarity. Bitachon is a heart-relationship, not an algorithm.

Source:
Chovot HaLevavot, Sha'ar HaBitachon, ch. 3

בְּיִרְאַת יְהֹוָה מִבְטַח עֹז וּלְבָנָיו יִהְיֶה מַחְסֶה

Transliteration: B'yirat Hashem mivtach oz, u'l'vanav yihiyeh machaseh; Mishlei 14:26

Translation: In fear of Hashem, is strong confidence, and for His children — a refuge.

Insight: The Tanya (Iggeret HaKodesh §22) notes that bitachon without yirah may turn into arrogance. But when trust is built on awe of Hashem, it becomes "oz" — indestructible strength that's inherited by one's children.

Source:
Tanya, Iggeret HaKodesh §22

בְּךָ בָּטְחוּ אֲבוֹתֵינוּ בָּטְחוּ וַתְּפַלְטֵמוֹ

Transliteration: Becha batchu avoteinu, batchu va-tefaltetemo

Translation: In You our fathers trusted — they trusted, and You delivered them.

Insight: The Shem MiShmuel (Beshalach 5670) explains: ancestral bitachon is an inheritance. If a Jew awakens trust, he accesses merit and power from generations before — Hashem doesn't allow that chain to be broken.

Source:
Shem MiShmuel, Beshalach 5670

בְּשָׁלוֹם יַחְדָּו אֶשְׁכְּבָה וְאִישָׁן כִּי אַתָּה יְהוָה לְבָדָד לָבֶטַח תּוֹשִׁיבֵנִי

Transliteration: B'shalom yachdav eshkavah ve'ishan, ki Atah Hashem levado la-vetach toshiveni; Tehillim 4:9

Translation: In peace together I lie down and sleep, for You alone, Hashem, settle me in security.

Insight: Rabbeinu Bachya (Kad HaKemach, Bitachon) writes: peace of mind, even in sleep, is the truest test of bitachon. The soul that surrenders at night shows whom it truly trusts.

Source:
Kad HaKemach, entry: Bitachon

בֵּאלֹהִים בָּטַחְתִּי לֹא אִירָא מַה יַּעֲשֶׂה בָשָׂר לִי

Transliteration: Be-Elokim batachti lo ira — mah ya'aseh basar li; Tehillim 56:5 / 12

Translation: In Elokim I have trusted; I will not fear. What can flesh do to me?

Insight: The Meshech Chochmah (Shemot 14:13) explains that this level of fearlessness comes only when a person detaches from the illusion that people control outcomes. "Basar" is powerless in the shadow of Divine decree.

Source:
Meshech Chochmah, Shemot 14:13

בֵּית אַהֲרֹן בִּטְחוּ בַיהוָה עֶזְרָם וּמָגִנָּם הוּא

Transliteration: Beit Aharon bitchu ba-Hashem, ezram u'maginam Hu; Tehillim 115:10

Translation: House of Aharon, trust in Hashem! He is their help and shield.

Insight: The Sfas Emes (Emor 5642) connects this verse to the Kohanim's avodah: their role as servants of the Mikdash is sustained only through trust. Their zechut is not from their lineage but their bitachon.

Source:
Sfas Emes, Emor 5642

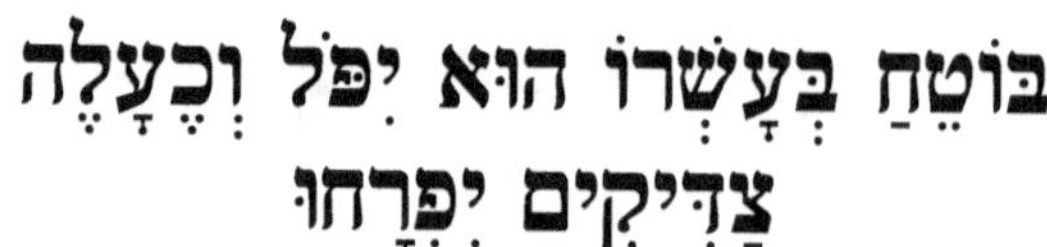

בּוֹטֵחַ בְּעָשְׁרוֹ הוּא יִפֹּל וְכֶעָלֶה
צַדִּיקִים יִפְרָחוּ

Transliteration: Bote'ach b'oshero hu yipol, ve'ke-aleh tzaddikim yifrachu; Mishlei 11:28

Translation: He who trusts in his wealth will fall, but the righteous will blossom like a leaf.

Insight: The Mesillat Yesharim (ch. 21) teaches that the danger of material success is self-reliance. But the tzaddik remains "like a leaf" humble, light, upward-reaching because his roots are in emunah, not economics.

Source:
Mesillat Yesharim, ch. 21

ג

Gimel
true bitachon is
solely in Hashem,
not in humans

גְּאוּלָה

גַּם אִישׁ שְׁלוֹמִי אֲשֶׁר בָּטַחְתִּי בוֹ,
אוֹכֵל לַחְמִי—הִגְדִּיל עָלַי עָקֵב.

Transliteration: Gam ish shelomi asher batachti bo, ochel lachmi—higdil alai akev. Tehillim 41:10

Translation: Even my ally in whom I trusted, who ate my bread, has raised his heel against me.

Insite: This verse expresses the pain of betrayal from one whom the speaker deeply trusted. The Midrash (Shocher Tov, Tehillim 41) explains that this can refer to moments of spiritual failure stemming from misplaced trust in people. Chazal teach that true bitachon—trust—must be solely in Hashem, not in human support (see Chovot HaLevavot, Sha'ar HaBitachon ch. 3).

Transliteration: Gol al Hashem darkecha, uvtach alav, ve'hu ya'aseh. Tehillim 37:5

Translation: Commit your way to Hashem, trust in Him, and He will act.

Insite: This is one of the foundations of bitachon. The Chazon Ish explains (Emunah U'Bitachon, ch. 2) that true trust does not mean expecting a specific outcome, but placing one's plans entirely in Hashem's hands and accepting whatever He does. The Zohar (Vayeishev 184a) notes that this level of surrender opens the gates of divine mercy, allowing Hashem to "do" in a way beyond nature.

Hay

Hashem is my salvation

הִנֵּה אֵ–ל יְשׁוּעָתִי; אֶבְטַח וְלֹא אֶפְחָד, כִּי עָזִּי וְזִמְרָת יָ–הּ יְהֹוָה; וַיְהִי לִי לִישׁוּעָה.

Transliteration: Hinei El yeshu'ati; evtach velo efchad, ki azi vezimrat Yah Hashem; vayehi li liyeshua. Yeshayahu 12:2

Translation: Behold, Hashem is my salvation; I will trust and not be afraid, for Hashem is my strength and my song, and He was my salvation.

Insite: The Seforno explains that emunah brings strength, and the awareness that Hashem is both protector and redeemer eliminates fear. The Noam Elimelech (Parshas Beshalach) teaches that "azi vezimrat Yah" implies that one who sings to Hashem through trust draws down salvation even before it manifests in this world.

הַשְׁמִיעֵנִי בַבֹּקֶר חַסְדֶּךָ, כִּי בְךָ בָטָחְתִּי; הוֹדִיעֵנִי דֶּרֶךְ זוּ אֵלֵךְ, כִּי אֵלֶיךָ נָשָׂאתִי נַפְשִׁי.

Transliteration: Hashmi'eni vaboker chasdecha ki vecha batachti; hodi'eni derech zu eilech, ki eilecha nasati nafshi. Tehillim 143:8

Translation: Let me hear Your kindness in the morning, for in You I trust; show me the path I should go, for I lift my soul to You.

Insite: According to the Ramchal (Mesilat Yesharim ch. 19), the morning represents clarity and freshness. Starting the day with bitachon invites Hashem's guidance throughout the entire path ahead. This pasuk is used in daily supplication by those who seek to live with Hashem's providence fully present.

Vav
Bitachon That Brings Peace and Redemption

וַיְהִי

וּבָטַחְתָּ כִּי יֵשׁ תִּקְוָה וְחָפַרְתָּ לָבֶטַח תִּשְׁכָּב. וְרָבַצְתָּ וְאֵין מַחֲרִיד וְחִלּוּ פָנֶיךָ רַבִּים.

Transliteration: U-vatachta ki yesh tikvah, ve-chafarta lavetach tishkav. Ve-ravatzta ve-ein macharid, ve-chillu fanecha rabbim. Iyov 11:18–19

Translation: You will trust because there is hope, and you will dig in security and lie down in peace. You will lie without fear, and many will seek your favor.

Insight: The Malbim interprets this as the natural outcome of spiritual clarity. One who lives with bitachon gains not only internal serenity but social strength. The Chazon Ish explains that true bitachon isn't about expecting outcomes it's about knowing that what will be is exactly what Hashem wants. That certainty gives rest to the soul.

Sources:
Malbim on Iyov 11

וְאַתָּה אֱלֹקִים תּוֹרִדֵם לִבְאֵר שַׁחַת,
אַנְשֵׁי דָמִים וּמִרְמָה לֹא יֶחֱצוּ יְמֵיהֶם;
וַאֲנִי אֶבְטַח בָּךְ.

Transliteration: Ve-atah Elokim toridem li-be'er shachat, anshei damim u-mirmah lo yechetz'u yemeihem; va-ani evtach bach. Tehillim 55:24

Translation: But You, Elokim, will bring them down to the pit of destruction; men of blood and deceit will not live out half their days. But I will trust in You.

Insight: This verse contrasts the fall of the wicked with the trust of the righteous. The Radak notes that while the deceitful shorten their lives through sin, the one who leans on Hashem transcends the fate of flesh. It's a declaration of confidence in divine justice over worldly power.

Source:
Radak on Tehillim 55:24

וַאֲנִי כְּזַיִת רַעֲנָן בְּבֵית אֱלֹקִים,
בָּטַחְתִּי בְחֶסֶד אֱלֹקִים עוֹלָם וָעֶד.

Transliteration: Va-ani ke-zayit ra'anan b'veit Elokim, batachti be-chesed Elokim olam va'ed. Tehillim 52:10

Translation: But I am like a fresh olive tree in the house of Elokim; I have trusted in the kindness of Elokim forever and ever.

Insight: The Sefat Emet teaches that the olive tree represents inner vitality — often crushed before it yields its oil. Trust in Hashem allows a person to remain rooted and fruitful, even when externally pressed. That trust is eternal, not situational.

Source:
Sefat Emet, Vayigash 5642

וְיִבְטְחוּ בְךָ יוֹדְעֵי שְׁמֶךָ, כִּי לֹא עָזַבְתָּ דֹרְשֶׁיךָ ה'.

Transliteration: Ve-yivtechu vecha yod'ei shemecha, ki lo azavta dorshecha Hashem. Tehillim 9:11

Translation: Those who know Your name will trust in You, for You have not forsaken those who seek You, Hashem.

Insight: Rabbeinu Yonah (Shaarei Teshuvah 3:30) writes that knowledge of Hashem's name implies intimate awareness of His kindness and reliability. The more one contemplates Hashem's past deeds, the more natural trust becomes.

Source:
Shaarei Teshuvah, 3:30

וַאֲנִי אָעֱנֶה חוֹרְפִי דָבָר, כִּי בָטַחְתִּי
בִדְבָרֶךָ.

Transliteration: Va-ani a'aneh chorfi davar, ki batachti bidvarecha. Tehillim 119:42

Translation: And I will respond to my mocker with a word, for I have trusted in Your word.

Insight: The Tanya (ch. 26) teaches that bitachon in Hashem's promise gives inner strength to stand against embarrassment and doubt. The response to shame is trust in the enduring truth of Torah, not in appeasing others.

Source:
Tanya, ch. 26

וַאֲנִי בְּחַסְדְּךָ בָטַחְתִּי, יָגֵל לִבִּי
בִּישׁוּעָתֶךָ, אָשִׁירָה לַה' כִּי גָמַל עָלָי.

Transliteration: Va-ani bechasdecha batachti; yagel libi bishuatecha, ashirah la-Hashem ki gamal alai.

Translation: But I have trusted in Your kindness; my heart will rejoice in Your salvation, I will sing to Hashem for He has dealt bountifully with me.

Insight: Rebbe Nachman of Breslov (Likutey Moharan II:7) taught that joy is the result of trust. The more one leans into Hashem's mercy, the more one can access simchah and song — even before salvation arrives.

Source:
Likutey Moharan, II:7

Transliteration: Va-yiten befI shir chadash, tehillah le-Elokeinu; yir'u rabbim v'yira'u, ve-yivtechu ba-Hashem. Tehillim 40:4

Translation: He placed in my mouth a new song, praise to our Elokim. Many will see and fear, and will trust in Hashem.

Insight: According to the Zohar (Vayikra 8a), a "new song" is not just a melody — it is a state of expanded consciousness that awakens others to emunah. When a tzaddik expresses joy from salvation, others are inspired to trust as well.

Source:
Zohar, Vayikra 8a

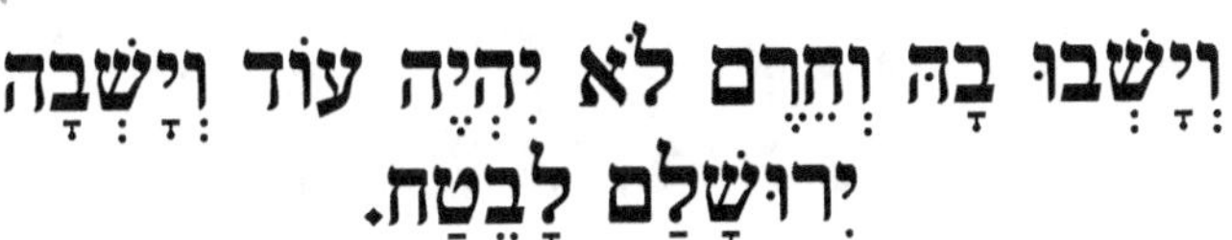

וְיָשְׁבוּ בָהּ וְחֵרֶם לֹא יִהְיֶה עוֹד וְיָשְׁבָה יְרוּשָׁלַם לָבֶטַח.

Transliteration: Veyashvu bah vecherem lo yihyeh od veyashvah Yerushalayim lavetach. Zecharia 14:11

Translation: And they shall dwell therein, and there shall be no more utter destruction; but Jerusalem shall dwell safely.

Insight: In this verse, the prophet Zechariah envisions a future where Jerusalem will be inhabited securely, free from the threat of destruction. From a Kabbalistic perspective, this signifies the rectification of the cosmic order, where the divine presence (Shechinah) is fully revealed, and the forces of impurity (Klipot) are subdued. The absence of "cherem" (utter destruction) symbolizes the removal of spiritual barriers that hinder the flow of divine light. Chassidic teachings interpret this as the culmination of the collective spiritual work of the Jewish people, leading to an era of peace and divine harmony.

Source: Sefer HaLikutim (Arizal) on Zechariah 14:11; Likutei Torah (Alter Rebbe), Vayechi 49:18.

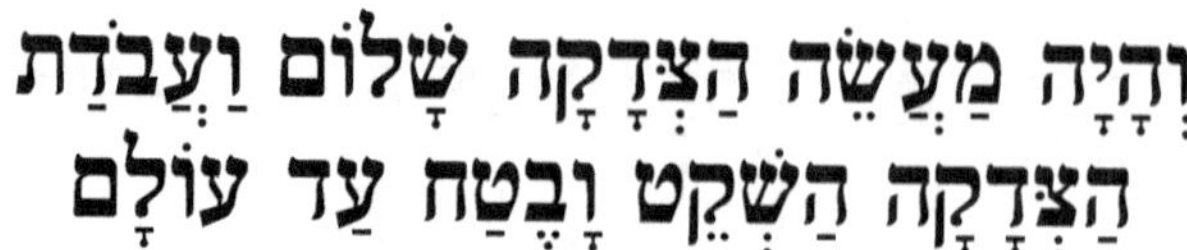

Transliteration: V'hayah ma'aseh ha'tzedakah shalom, va'avodat ha'tzedakah hashket va'vetach ad olam. Yishayahu 32:17

Translation: And the work of righteousness will be peace, and the service of righteousness—quietness and security forever.

Insight: The Shinover Rebbe explains that "tzedakah" (righteousness or charity) is not only about giving but about aligning the soul with the divine attribute of Chesed (loving-kindness). When man performs mitzvos with pure intention, he draws peace into all worlds. The "quiet and security" referenced here are reflections of inner stillness — when the soul is no longer pulled by confusion or fear. According to the Ramchal (Derech Hashem, I:4:6), such inner alignment allows divine light to flow without resistance, manifesting in lasting tranquility.

Source:
Divrei Yechezkel (Shinov), parshas Mishpatim;
Derech Hashem I:4:6

Transliteration: Veyashvu ish tachat gafno v'tachat te'enato ve'ein macharid. Micha 4:4

Translation: And each man shall sit under his vine and under his fig tree, and no one will make them afraid.

Insight: The Sefas Emes interprets the vine and fig tree as metaphors for Torah (gafen) and mitzvos (te'enah). Sitting beneath them suggests internalization — not merely observing commandments but resting in them. Fearlessness comes when one's inner world is nourished by divine truth.

The Meor Einayim (Chernobyl) adds that when a person is rooted in his unique purpose (shoresh nishmaso), he finds peace even in a turbulent world — thus, "no one will make them afraid."

Source:
Sefas Emes, Vayigash 5641;
Meor Einayim, Va'eschanan

וַעֲשִׂיתֶם אֹתָם וִישַׁבְתֶּם לָבֶטַח בְּאַרְצְכֶם.
וְנָתַתִּי שָׁלוֹם בָּאָרֶץ
וּשְׁכַבְתֶּם וְאֵין מַחֲרִיד

Transliteration: Va'asitem otam, v'yishavtem lavetach b'artz'chem. Ve'natati shalom ba'aretz u'shchavtem ve'ein macharid. Vayikra 26:3-6

Translation: And you shall do them (My laws), and you will dwell securely in your land. And I will give peace in the land, and you shall lie down, and none shall make you afraid.

Insight: The Kedushas Levi teaches that when mitzvos are done with joy and sincerity — not by rote — they awaken upper worlds to shower peace below. The promise here is not just political peace, but the ability to "lie down" — to rest, knowing your soul is aligned with its purpose. Rabbeinu Yonah in Shaarei Teshuvah writes that real security is when a person trusts in Hashem's justice and mercy; only then does fear dissolve.

Source:
Kedushas Levi, Bechukosai;
Rabbeinu Yonah, Shaar HaBitachon

וַיִּשְׁכֹּן יִשְׂרָאֵל בֶּטַח בָּדָד עֵין יַעֲקֹב אֶל אֶרֶץ דָּגָן וְתִירוֹשׁ אַף שָׁמָיו יַעַרְפוּ טָל

Transliteration: Va'yishkon Yisrael betach badad, ein Yaakov el eretz dagan ve'tirosh; af shamayav ya'arfu tal. Devarim 33:28

Translation: And Israel shall dwell in security, alone, the eye of Jacob [turned] to a land of grain and wine; even his heavens shall drop dew.

Insight: The Or HaChaim HaKadosh explains that "betach badad" (secure and alone) reflects a spiritual independence — when Israel looks only to Hashem and not to worldly powers. Then the land responds with abundance, both physically and spiritually.
Rebbe Nachman (Likutei Moharan I:22) sees "dew" (tal) as a metaphor for divine insight that nourishes the soul in hidden ways — when a person is truly in bitachon, he receives inspiration from realms beyond logic.

Source:
Or HaChaim, Devarim 33:28;
Likutei Moharan I:22

Zaien

Only in One do we Trust

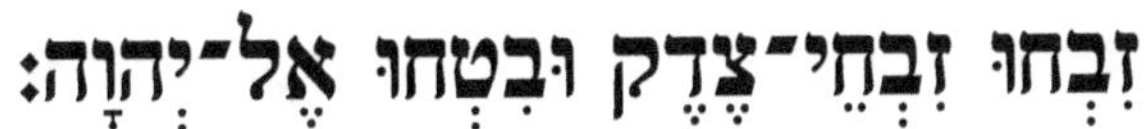

Transliteration: Ziv'chu zivchei-tzedek u'vitchu el Hashem. Tehillim 4:6

Translation: Offer righteous sacrifices and trust in Hashem.

Insight: According to the Zohar (Vayikra 8a), a "righteous sacrifice" refers not only to animal offerings but also to the internal sacrifice of ego and selfish desire. Trust in Hashem perfects the offering, elevating it beyond the physical to the spiritual realm.

Source:
Zohar Vayikra 8a;
Mesilas Yesharim, ch. 19

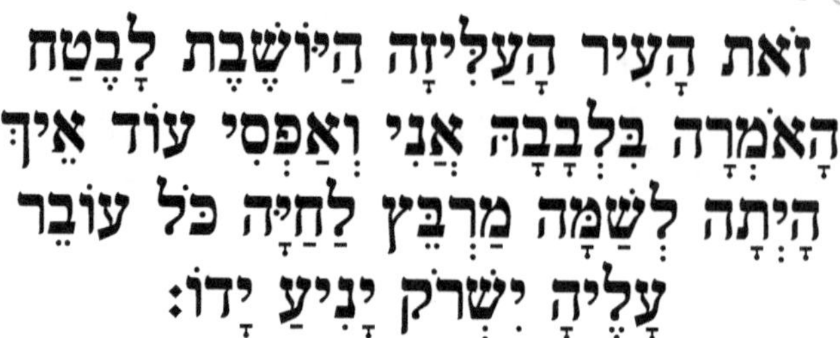

Transliteration: Zot Ha`ir Ha`aleezah hayoshevet lavetach haomrah bilvava ani ve`afsi od eich hayta lshama mrbetz kchaya col over ahleha yishrok yonia yado . Tzfania 2:15

Translation: This is the joyful city, dwelling securely, saying, "I am, and there is none besides me." How did it become desolate, a resting place for the beasts? everyone who passes by her shall wistle and wave his hand.

Insight: The Ramchal writes that when a person truly makes Hashem his dwelling, meaning he lives with constant awareness of Hashem, he reaches a level of bitachon (trust) where he is no longer affected by external chaos.

Source:
Ramchal, Daas Tevunos §162;
Zohar Terumah 161b

ח

Chet

Trust in the Kindness of Hashem

חֶֽסֶד

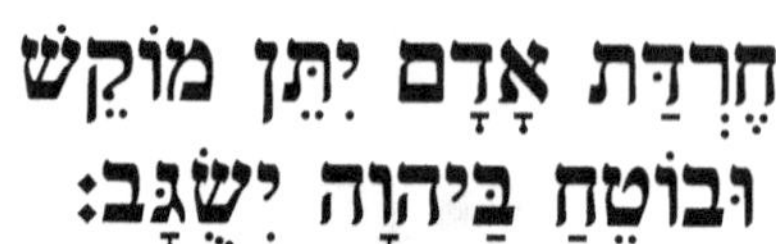

Transliteration: Cherdat adam yiten mokesh, u'voteach ba'Hashem yesugav. Mishlei 29:25

Translation: Fear of man is a trap, but whoever trusts in Hashem will be elevated.

Insight: The Chovos HaLevavos teaches that fear of others reflects inner doubt, whereas true trust (bitachon) elevates the soul, aligning it with divine clarity. The word yesugav implies spiritual transcendence.

Source:
Chovos HaLevavos,
Shaar HaBitachon, ch. 1

Tet

Everything Hashem does is Good

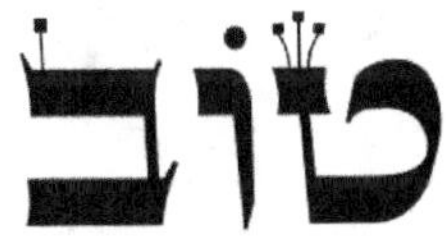

טוֹב לַחֲסוֹת בַּיהוָה מִבְּטֹחַ בָּאָדָם:
טוֹב לַחֲסוֹת בַּיהוָה מִבְּטֹחַ בִּנְדִיבִים:

Transliteration: Tov lachasot ba'Hashem mi'vtach ba'adam. Tov lachasot ba'Hashem mi'vtach b'nedivim. Tehillim 118:8–9

Translation: It is better to take refuge in Hashem than to trust in man. It is better to take refuge in Hashem than to trust in nobles.

Insight: According to Rebbe Nachman of Breslov, trusting people (even princes) is limited by their mortality. Trusting Hashem connects you to the Ein Sof, which is beyond nature and time.

Source:
Likutei Moharan I:62

י

Yud

*Hashem shines
His countenance
upon the world*

יִשְׂרָאֵל בְּטַח בַּיהוָה עֶזְרָם וּמָגִנָּם הוּא:

Transliteration: Yisrael, betach ba'Hashem; ezram u'maginam hu. Tehillim 115:9

Translation: Israel, trust in Hashem; He is their help and their shield.

Insight: The Sfas Emes explains that "help and shield" means Hashem supports both internally (help) and externally (protection). Trust unlocks both aspects.

Source:
Sfas Emes, Parshas Bechukosai 5643

יְהֹוָה עֻזִּי וּמָגִנִּי בּוֹ בָטַח לִבִּי וְנֶעֱזָרְתִּי וַיַּעֲלֹז לִבִּי וּמִשִּׁירִי אֲהוֹדֶנּוּ׃

Transliteration: Hashem uzi u'magini, bo batach libi ve'ne'ezarti, va'yaaloz libi u'mishiri ahodenu. Tehillim 28:7

Translation: Hashem is my strength and my shield; my heart trusted in Him, and I was helped; so my heart exults, and with my song I will praise Him.

Insight: Rabbi Tzadok HaKohen teaches that when the heart truly trusts in Hashem, even before salvation arrives, joy already enters — because the connection itself is redemptive.

Source:
Tzidkas HaTzaddik §143

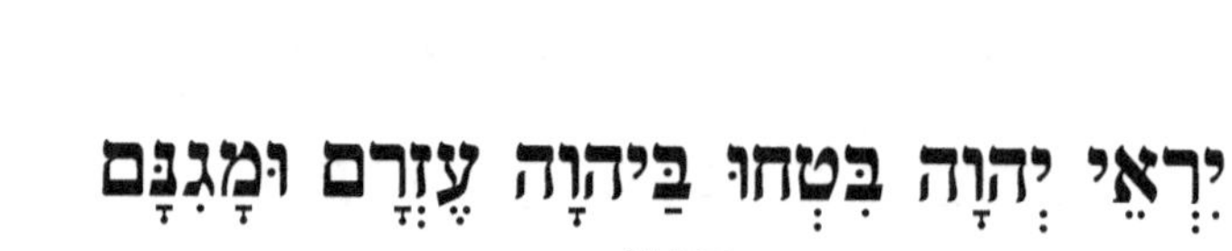

יִרְאֵי יְהוָה בִּטְחוּ בַּיהוָה עֶזְרָם וּמָגִנָּם
הוּא

Transliteration: Yir'ei Hashem, bitchu ba'Hashem; ezram u'maginam hu. Tehillim 115:11

Translation: Those who fear Hashem, trust in Hashem; He is their help and their shield.

Insight: The Mesilas Yesharim explains that awe (yirah) alone can paralyze a person unless balanced by trust (bitachon). Only with both does one walk upright in divine service.

Source:
Mesilas Yesharim, ch. 24

יוֹם אִירָא אֲנִי אֵלֶיךָ אֶבְטָח

Transliteration: Yom ira ani eilecha evtach.
Tehillim 56:4

Translation: On the day I fear, I will trust in You.

Insight: Fear and trust are not opposites — fear can be the very trigger that leads to trust. The Chazon Ish writes that fear reveals our limitations, while trust reconnects us to the unlimited.

Source:
Chazon Ish, Emunah u'Bitachon, ch. 2

יֵצֶר סָמוּךְ תִּצֹּר שָׁלוֹם שָׁלוֹם כִּי בְךָ בָּטוּחַ

Transliteration: Yetzer samuch titzor shalom shalom, ki vecha batuach. Yeshayahu (Isaiah) 26:3

Translation: You will keep in perfect peace one whose mind is steadfast, because he trusts in You.

Insight: The Ari Z"l teaches that the repetition "shalom shalom" refers to peace in both the upper and lower worlds — granted to the one whose thoughts are "samuch" (resting, supported) on Hashem.

Source:
Eitz Chaim, Shaar Rosh HaShanah, Derush 1

Kaf

Hashem is the
King of all kings

כֹּה אָמַר יְהֹוָה: אָרוּר הַגֶּבֶר אֲשֶׁר יִבְטַח בָּאָדָם וְשָׂם בָּשָׂר זְרֹעוֹ, וּמִן יְהֹוָה יָסוּר לִבּוֹ

Transliteration: Ko amar Hashem: Arur ha'gever asher yivtach ba'adam ve'sam basar z'ro'o, u'min Hashem yasur libo. Yirmiyahu 17:5

Translation: Thus says Hashem: Cursed is the man who trusts in man and makes flesh his strength, and whose heart turns away from Hashem.

Insight: This verse warns against placing ultimate reliance on human beings or material power. According to the Zohar (Beshalach 61a), such trust "cuts the connection" to the supernal flow of divine sustenance. The Sfas Emes explains that trust in flesh (human effort alone) narrows spiritual consciousness, while bitachon in Hashem opens access to deeper realities.

Source:
Zohar Beshalach 61a;
Sfas Emes, Parshas Bechukosai 5642

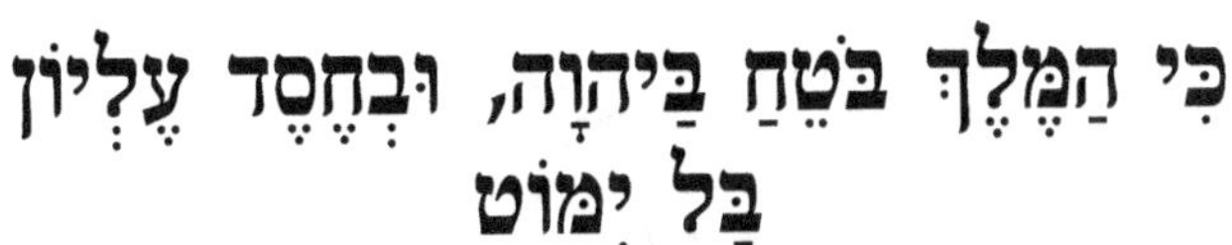

כִּי הַמֶּלֶךְ בֹּטֵחַ בַּיהֹוָה, וּבְחֶסֶד עֶלְיוֹן
בַּל יִמּוֹט

Transliteration: Ki ha-melekh bote'ach ba'Hashem, u'v'chesed Elyon bal yimot. Tehillim 21:8

Translation: For the king trusts in Hashem, and through the kindness of the Most High, he shall not falter.

Insight: The Malbim explains that the king's stability doesn't come from political might but from divine kindness (chesed Elyon). The Kedushas Levi sees this as a model for leadership: a leader must be grounded in bitachon to merit divine support that never wavers.

Source:
Malbim on Tehillim 21:8;
Kedushas Levi, Parshas Shoftim

כִּי בוֹ יִשְׂמַח לִבֵּנוּ, כִּי בְשֵׁם קָדְשׁוֹ בָטָחְנוּ

Transliteration: Ki vo yismach libeinu, ki v'shem kodsho batachnu. Tehillim 33:21

Translation: For in Him our heart shall rejoice, because we have trusted in His holy name.

Insight: Joy is not a result of circumstances, but a byproduct of trust in Hashem's holiness. The Me'or Einayim writes that "trust in the holy name" is not abstract—it means to live with awareness that every event is part of Hashem's unity (achdus), which brings inner joy even in concealment.

Source:
Me'or Einayim, Parshas Va'eira

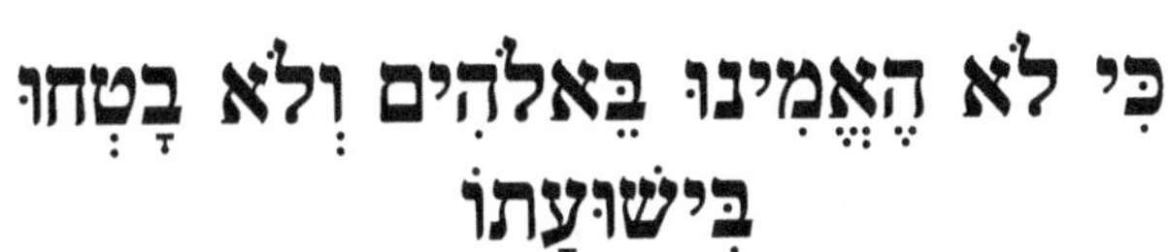

כִּי לֹא הֶאֱמִינוּ בֵּאלֹהִים וְלֹא בָטְחוּ בִּישׁוּעָתוֹ

Transliteration: Ki lo he'eminu b'Elokim ve'lo batchu b'yeshuato. Tehillim 78:22

Translation: For they did not believe in God and did not trust in His salvation.

Insight: The Ohr HaChaim HaKadosh teaches that lack of trust blocks the light of redemption. Even when salvation is prepared, it cannot be revealed without the vessel of emunah and bitachon.

Source:
Ohr HaChaim, Parshas Beshalach

כְּמוֹהֶם יִהְיוּ עֹשֵׂיהֶם, כֹּל אֲשֶׁר בֹּטֵחַ בָּהֶם

Transliteration: K'mohem yihyu oseihem, kol asher bote'ach bahem. Tehillim 115:8

Translation: Those who make them will become like them—everyone who trusts in them.

Insight: This is said about idol-makers and their worshippers. The Meshech Chochmah writes that trust defines identity: one who trusts in lifeless things becomes spiritually dull. Conversely, trusting in Hashem enlivens the soul.

Source:
Meshech Chochmah, Parshas Yisro

כִּי אַתָּה תִקְוָתִי אֲדֹנָי יְהוִה מִבְטַחִי מִנְּעוּרָי

Transliteration: Ki Atah tikvati, Adonai Hashem, mivtachi min'urai. Tehillim 71:5

Translation: For You are my hope, Hashem, my trust from my youth.

Insight: The Tanya (Iggeres HaKodesh 11) explains that "hope" and "trust" are not passive feelings—they are rooted in daas, the inner awareness that Hashem is the sole source of support. A lifelong relationship with trust in Hashem brings consistency through all life stages.

Source:
Tanya, Iggeres HaKodesh §11

כִּי לֹא בְקַשְׁתִּי אֶבְטָח וְחַרְבִּי לֹא תוֹשִׁיעֵנִי

Transliteration: Ki lo v'kashti evtach, ve'charbi lo toshi'eini. Tehillim 44:7

Translation: For I do not trust in my bow, and my sword will not save me.

Insight: This is a declaration of bitachon in the midst of battle. The Chazon Ish teaches that one must use natural means (like sword and bow), but not place their trust in them. True bitachon is when one's heart is calm because trust is placed only in Hashem.

Source:
Chazon Ish, Emunah u'Bitachon ch. 2

Lamed

Hashem wants
our hearts

לְדָוִד שָׁפְטֵנִי יְהוָה כִּי אֲנִי בְּתֻמִּי
הָלַכְתִּי, וּבַיהוָה בָּטַחְתִּי לֹא אֶמְעָד

Transliteration: LeDovid, shofteini Hashem ki ani b'tumi halachti, u'vaHashem batachti, lo emad. Tehillim 26:1

Translation: Of David: Judge me, Hashem, for I have walked in my integrity, and I have trusted in Hashem—I shall not falter.

Insight: According to the Noam Elimelech, "walking in integrity" (tumah) is not self-righteousness, but humility that stems from full trust in Hashem. When one walks in temimus, he is no longer relying on his own merit but on divine guidance. Trust (bitachon) ensures spiritual steadiness, because the soul no longer trembles from external instability.

Source:
Noam Elimelech, Parshas Toldos;
Likutei Halachos, Birchas HaPeiros 5:7

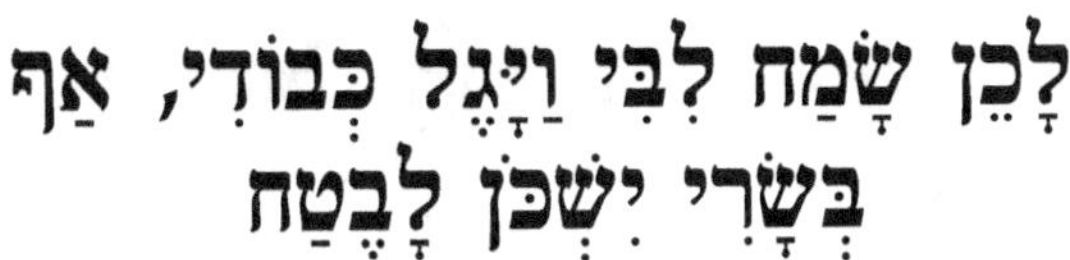

לָכֵן שָׂמַח לִבִּי וַיָּגֶל כְּבוֹדִי, אַף בְּשָׂרִי יִשְׁכֹּן לָבֶטַח

Transliteration: Lachein samach libi, va'yagel kevodi, af b'sari yishkon lavetach. Tehillim 16:9

Translation: Therefore, my heart is glad, and my glory rejoices; even my flesh shall dwell in security.

Insight: The Chiddushei HaRim teaches that "my heart" symbolizes emotional trust, "my glory" is the soul, and "my flesh" is the body. When trust in Hashem penetrates deeply enough to cause joy (simchah), it flows from soul to body. Bitachon isn't only spiritual—it brings physical peace as well.

Source: Chiddushei HaRim,
    Tehillim 16:9;
    Tanya,
    Iggeres HaKodesh §11

לְבִנְיָמִן אָמַר: יְדִיד יְהֹוָה יִשְׁכֹּן לָבֶטַח עָלָיו חֹפֵף, עָלָיו כָּל הַיּוֹם, וּבֵין כְּתֵפָיו שָׁכֵן

Transliteration: Le'Vinyamin amar: Yedid Hashem yishkon lavetach alav chofef, alav kol ha'yom, u'vein kteifav shachein. Devarim 33:12

Translation: Of Binyamin he said: The beloved of Hashem shall dwell securely beside Him; He shelters him all day long, and dwells between his shoulders.

Insight: According to the Zohar (Vayechi 226a), Binyamin symbolizes the inner dwelling of the Shechinah. "Between his shoulders" represents the Beis HaMikdash resting in his territory. But mystically, this verse speaks of every soul: one who becomes beloved through bitachon merits to have Hashem dwell within.

Source: Zohar I 226a;
Shem MiShmuel,
Parshas V'Zos HaBracha

Mem

Hashem is with us always

מַשְׂכִּיל עַל־דָּבָר יִמְצָא טוֹב; וּבוֹטֵחַ בַּה' אַשְׁרָיו

Transliteration: Maskil al davar yimtza tov; u'vote'ach ba'Hashem ashreihu. Mishlei 16:20

Translation: A discerning person will find good; and one who trusts in Hashem—fortunate is he.

Insight: The Vilna Gaon teaches that true insight (haskalah) means knowing how to live in line with divine wisdom. When this knowledge is coupled with trust in Hashem, it leads to lasting goodness—both spiritual and physical. According to Rabbeinu Yonah, trusting in Hashem is itself the greatest good a person can attain, and brings happiness regardless of circumstance.

Source:
Vilna Gaon on Mishlei 16:20;
Shaarei Teshuvah 3:32

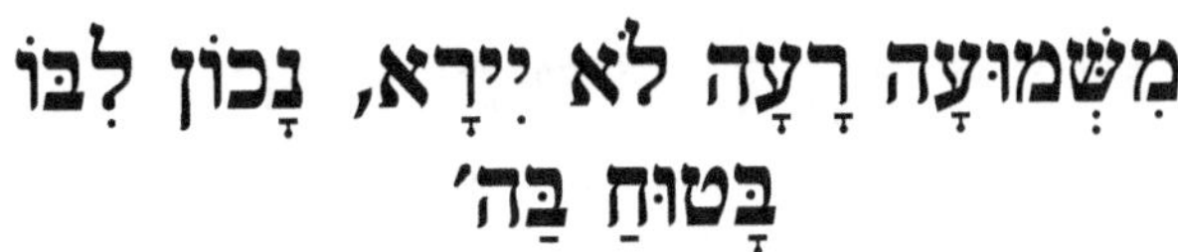

מִשְּׁמוּעָה רָעָה לֹא יִירָא, נָכוֹן לִבּוֹ בָּטוּחַ בַּה׳

Transliteration: Mi'shemuah ra'ah lo yira; nachon libo batuach ba'Hashem. Tehillim 112:7

Translation: He will not fear bad news; his heart is steadfast, trusting in Hashem.

Insight: The Sfas Emes explains: when a person's heart is fixed in bitachon, no external fear can shake him. Even "bad news" does not break his inner alignment, because he sees all events as from Hashem. This emotional stability is a fruit of deep spiritual work.

Source:
Sfas Emes, Tehillim 112

מִי בָכֶם יְרֵא ה׳ שֹׁמֵעַ בְּקוֹל עַבְדּוֹ
אֲשֶׁר הָלַךְ חֲשֵׁכִים וְאֵין נֹגַהּ לוֹ; יִבְטַח
בְּשֵׁם ה׳ וְיִשָּׁעֵן בֵּאלֹהָיו

Transliteration: Mi bakhem yerei Hashem shomea b'kol avdo, asher halach chasheichim ve'ein nogah lo; yivtach b'shem Hashem ve'yisha'en b'Elokav. Yeshayahu 50:10

Translation: Who among you fears Hashem, listens to the voice of His servant, yet walks in darkness with no light? Let him trust in the name of Hashem and rely upon his God.

Insight: The Malbim writes that even a G-d-fearing person can experience spiritual darkness. The path forward is trust. According to Tanya (Iggeres HaKodesh 11), bitachon during hester panim (divine concealment) is the highest level of connection, for it comes without reassurance only faith.

Source:
Malbim on Yeshayahu 50:10;
Tanya, Iggeres HaKodesh §11

Nun

Hashem is faithful to His word

נוֹרָאוֹת בְּצֶדֶק תַּעֲנֵנוּ אֱלֹקֵי יִשְׁעֵנוּ
מִבְטָח כָּל קַצְוֵי־אֶרֶץ וְיָם רְחֹקִים

Transliteration: Nora'ot b'tzedek ta'anenu, Elokei yisheinu; mivtach kol katzei aretz v'yam rechokim. Tehillim 65:6

Translation: With awesome deeds of righteousness You answer us, O G-d of our salvation—the trust of all ends of the earth and far-off seas.

Insight: The Radak sees this as global recognition that Hashem is the true source of salvation. In Chassidus, the "far-off seas" refer to distant souls, who despite spiritual distance, still place trust in Hashem—this trust itself brings them near.

Source:
Radak on Tehillim 65:6;
Degel Machaneh Ephraim, Va'eira

נָסֹגוּ אָחוֹר יֵבֹשׁוּ בֹשֶׁת הַבֹּטְחִים
בַּפָּסֶל הָאֹמְרִים לְמַסֵּכָה אַתֶּם אֱלֹקֵינוּ

Transliteration: Nisogu achor, yevoshu boshet ha'botchim ba'fesel, ha'omrim l'masseicha: atem Elokeinu. Tehillim 97:7

Translation: They will retreat in shame—those who trust in idols, who say to molten images: "You are our gods."

Insight: The Mesilas Yesharim teaches that trust must be placed only in the One who has power. Trusting in any other force—even unconsciously—disconnects one from divine flow. Shame here reflects the spiritual emptiness of misplaced trust.

Source:
Mesilas Yesharim, ch. 19

Riesh

Hashem does the will of those that fear Him

רַבִּים מַכְאֹבִים לָרָשָׁע, וְהַבּוֹטֵחַ בַּה'
חֶסֶד יְסוֹבְבֶנּוּ

Transliteration: Rabim mach'ovim la'rasha, ve'ha'bote'ach ba'Hashem, chesed y'sovevenu. Tehillim 32:10

Translation: Many are the sorrows of the wicked, but one who trusts in Hashem—kindness surrounds him.

Insight: The Ohr HaChaim notes that even without merit, one who trusts in Hashem is enveloped by chesed. Trust doesn't just earn reward—it draws divine grace that transcends judgment.

Source:
Ohr HaChaim, Shemos 14:31;
Zohar II 184a

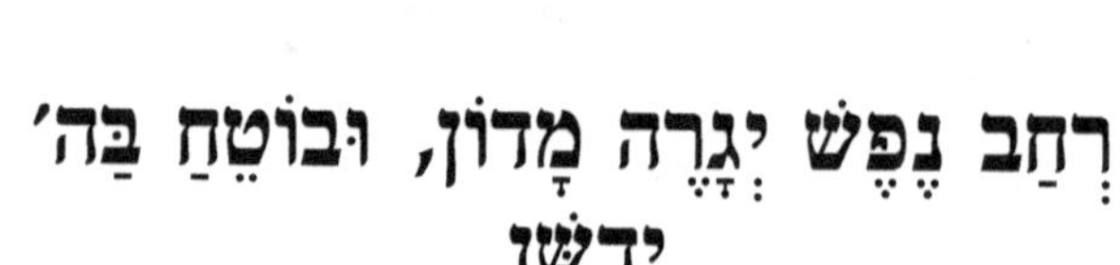

רְחַב נֶפֶשׁ יְגָרֶה מָדוֹן, וּבוֹטֵחַ בַּה׳
יְדֻשָּׁן:

Transliteration: Rechav nefesh yegareh madon, u'voteach ba'Hashem yedushan

Translation: One with a greedy soul stirs up strife, but one who trusts in Hashem will be enriched.

Insight: The Chida explains that lack of trust leads to jealousy and conflict; but trust brings serenity and abundance. "Yedushan" (shall be enriched) is both material and spiritual.

Source:
Chida, Nachal Kedumim on Mishlei 28:25

שׁ

Shin

Hashem Protects us

שׁוֹמֵר יִשְׂרָאֵל

שָׁמְרָה נַפְשִׁי כִּי חָסִיד אָנִי, הוֹשַׁע
עַבְדְּךָ אַתָּה אֱלֹקַי, הַבּוֹטֵחַ אֵלֶיךָ

Transliteration: Sh'morah nafshi ki chassid ani, hosha avdecha, Atah Elokai, ha'bote'ach eilecha. Tehillim 86:2

Translation: Guard my soul, for I am devoted; save Your servant—You are my God, the one who trusts in You.

Insight: The Rebbe of Slonim explains that a true chassid isn't one who is perfect, but one who places his entire being in Hashem's hands. That trust itself is what makes one worthy of protection.

Source:
Netivot Shalom, Tehillim 86

שִׁיר הַמַּעֲלוֹת: הַבּוֹטְחִים בַּה׳ כְּהַר צִיּוֹן, לֹא יִמּוֹט לְעוֹלָם יֵשֵׁב

Transliteration: Shir ha'ma'alos: ha'botchim ba'Hashem ke'har Tzion, lo yimot, l'olam yeshev. Tehillim 125:1

Translation: A Song of Ascents: Those who trust in Hashem are like Mount Zion, which cannot be shaken, and will dwell forever.

Insight: The Baal Shem Tov teaches that bitachon makes a person unshakable—not because the world doesn't tremble, but because his inner core is anchored in the eternal.

Source:
Tzava'as HaRivash §70; Likutei Moharan I:260

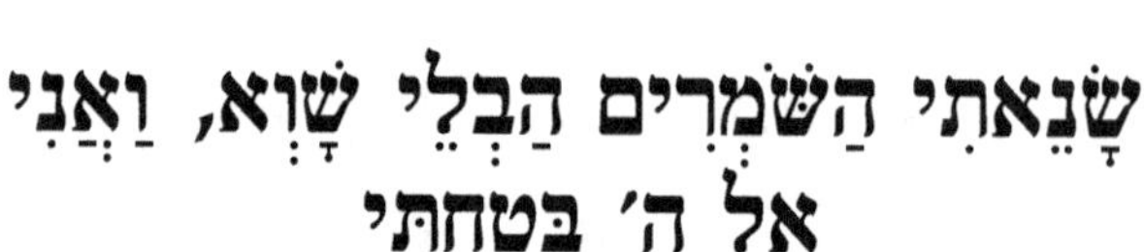

שָׂנֵאתִי הַשֹּׁמְרִים הַבְלֵי שָׁוְא, וַאֲנִי אֶל ה' בָּטָחְתִּי

Transliteration: Saneti ha'shomrim havlei shav, va'ani el Hashem batachti. Tehillim 31:7

Translation: I hate those who cling to worthless vanities, but I have trusted in Hashem.

Insight: Trust in Hashem is not just belief—it's a choice to reject false securities. The Ramban says this verse reflects full bitul (self-nullification), because trusting Hashem means letting go of all illusions of control.

Source:
Ramban, Emunah U'Bitachon ch. 1

How to Attain Supernatural Powers through the Torah

Based on פרקי מחשבה of Rav Yaakov Addes Slit''a

How to Attain Supernatural Powers through to Torah

Based on the teachings of Rav Yaakov Addes Slit''a

Introduction

In a world fascinated by supernatural abilities, the Torah offers a perspective deeply rooted in spiritual discipline, kedushah (holiness), and deveikus (cleaving to Hashem). The idea of transcending the natural order is not foreign to Chazal (our Sages), nor to the mekubalim (Kabbalists), but the path is one of avodat Hashem and inner refinement.

The Hidden Desire
Awakened by Something Higher

You've Felt It Before

There are moments in life when something stirs inside us that can't be explained rationally. It might happen beside a hospital bed. Or at a funeral. Or in the silence of a Friday night with candles flickering and nothing but breath and memory in the air. Sometimes it strikes during a sunrise in the desert or in the sudden realization that a verse you once heard as a child carries weight, mystery, and fire.

In those moments, something wakes up inside you. You feel a whisper—sometimes loud, sometimes gentle—pulling you to more. Not more success, more comfort, or more pleasure. But more meaning. More connection. Something larger than yourself. Something beyond the surface. Something supernatural.

If you've ever felt that, even for a second, you're already halfway through the gate. The rest of this article is for those who don't want that moment to pass by forgotten.

The Jewish Soul is Wired for the Infinite

According to the deepest teachings of Torah and Kabbalah, the Jewish soul is not a passive spark. It is an active flame. It is not only created by Hashem—it is part of the Divine flow itself. And because of that, it is capable of reaching levels that defy the laws of nature.

This idea isn't poetry. It's a foundational truth repeated over and over in the works of the Arizal, the Ramchal, and countless others:

The soul is not just spiritual—it is holy, luminous, and embedded with a yearning that does not die.

Even when buried beneath layers of sin, trauma, cynicism, or doubt, it never loses its power.

Every time a Jew feels a sudden urge to do good, or feels pain over their distance from Torah, or feels inexplicably pulled to truth or teshuvah— it is not an illusion. It is the neshama calling. And when one answers, even a little, it activates a chain reaction in the upper worlds.

You Were Not Made for Smallness

Modern life is very good at shrinking us. Even when we're "succeeding," most of us live with a quiet sense of emptiness, as if we are playing in a sandbox while the gates of a vast palace sit locked beside us. We become numb to holiness. Prayer feels dry. Torah feels distant. We don't expect to ever feel awe. We settle for small pleasures, hoping it will dull the ache.

But Torah doesn't accept that smallness.

Torah teaches that every single Jew, regardless of background, baggage, or mistakes, carries within them a direct connection—the same power that split the sea, spoke at Sinai, and sustains all reality from second to second.

And here is the bold claim of this path:

You do not need to become someone else to access the supernatural. You only need to become who you already are at the root.

Supernatural Doesn't Mean Superficial

Let's be clear: when Torah talks about supernatural powers, it doesn't mean X-ray vision or walking through walls. It refers to the capacity to live in a state where your presence alters reality—where prayer changes outcomes, where your Torah learning literally repairs broken places in the spiritual structure of the world, where your inner clarity can illuminate others without speaking.

According to Torah, every Jew is born with this potential. Not an elite few. Not tzaddikim only. Not just mystics. Everyone.

You are meant to live as someone who is not bound by what your eyes can see.

Why Haven't You Felt It?

So why do we feel so far from this? Why do most people, even religious ones, live their entire lives without ever touching this depth?

Because it's buried. And it's buried under layers that were put there—some by our own choices, some by trauma, some by design.

The soul, the Kabbalists teach, is surrounded by "klipot"—shells, layers of distortion. They don't destroy the soul. They just cover it. And those layers make us believe the lie that we are ordinary, that we are static, that we are powerless. But the power is not gone. It's waiting.

And sometimes, it takes only a single honest moment of humility, of yearning, of learning, to pierce through and let the brilliant light start to shine.

This Isn't Inspiration. This Is Structure.

The teachings we're about to explore are not feel-good ideas. They are frameworks used for centuries by sages who walked with Hashem, by people who lit up rooms and healed others with their presence, who moved Heaven and Earth with words alone.

Their tools are available. The laws are known. The system is here.

The only thing you need is to want it.

If something inside you is whispering right now, "I know this is true," then you've already begun. In the next section, we'll begin to explore the mechanisms: what the soul is made of, how mitzvot and Torah learning generate spiritual power, and what blocks that power from flowing.

But for now, pause. Ask yourself:
Do you believe it's possible for a human being to live in direct relationship with Hashem, and not be bound by the limits of this world?

The Architecture of the Soul – How Torah Generates Spiritual Power

The Soul Is Not a Symbol. It's a System.

For many people, the word "soul" is vague something poetic, something moral, maybe something mystical. But in Torah thought especially in the works of the Arizal, the Ramchal, and Rav Chaim Vital, the soul is not symbolic. It is a structured, layered, and fully functional system of spirituality. It is a real entity with defined channels, energy centers (ten sefirot), and direct connections to the upper worlds.

Every mitzvah you perform, every word of Torah you learn, even the smallest thought you direct toward holiness—these are not simply good deeds. They are spiritual actions that activate parts of your soul and send waves of influence upward into the upper infrastructure of the universe.

This is not a metaphor. This is spiritual physics.

You Are a Channel for Divine Energy

Let's begin with one of the boldest and most repeated ideas in Torah mysticism:
The soul of a Jew is "a portion of Hashem from above" *(as quoted in many sefarim, including Tanya and the writings of the Arizal).*

That means Hashem does not just create your soul; the light of Hashem is drawn to the inner aspect of your soul.

When you act in alignment with Torah—when you learn, pray, give tzedakah, or even hold back from sin—you're not just improving your character. You are aligning your inner system with Hashem's will, which allows a flow of abundance known as shefa to move through your soul into the world.

This flow can bring wisdom, Healing, Strength, and Clarity. Even changes in the physical world. It is what the Kabbalists describe as "drawing light from the upper worlds into the lower."

When you learn Torah, for example, you aren't just "studying." You are acting like a spiritual antenna; receiving, translating, and transmitting Divine blessings into the world.

Torah Is More Than Knowledge. It's Spiritual Electricity.

Rav Yaakov Addes Slit"a (author of the sefer this part of the book is based on) explains again and again: Torah learning creates real change. It repairs spiritual worlds, strengthens your neshama, and elevates the total spiritual environment of Am Yisrael. He describes Torah as a power source—a sacred fire that illuminates your soul and transmits holiness into all layers of reality.

Even one moment of Torah study, done sincerely, can "move the heavens," as he writes.

Even one verse learned with intention can generate a wave of spiritual light that travels through the soul upward into the Sefirot.

And not only that—the soul itself expands in response to learning. Its channels widen. Its awareness deepens. It becomes more refined, more intuitive, more capable of perceiving holiness.

Mitzvot Are Not External Rituals.
They're Soul-Building Codes.

Every mitzvah, according to Kabbalistic writings, activates a specific dimension of the soul. The 613 mitzvot are not random obligations. They are spiritual keys. Each one opens a gate. Each one unlocks or strengthens a part of the world.

The soul has five primary levels (Nefesh, Ruach, Neshamah, Chayah, Yechidah), and mitzvot correspond to these levels in different ways. They cleanse, connect, empower, and protect.

When mitzvot are done without awareness, the power is still present—but when they're done with kavannah (conscious intention), the effect is exponential. The soul doesn't just passively receive—it transforms.

Sin Is Not Just Failure. It's Spiritual Sabotage.

Just as mitzvot build and elevate the soul, aveirot (sins) block the flow of spiritual energy. They "clog the pipes," so to speak. They create distortions and barriers that restrict the light from flowing freely.

Even worse, some sins open your system to external forces—what Kabbalistic texts call koach ha-tumah (forces of impurity). These forces are real and hungry. They feed on spiritual energy, and the moment you open a gate—through anger, pride, lust, dishonesty—they begin to siphon your strength.

That's why the Arizal taught that one of the biggest reasons the yetzer hara fights so hard to make you sin is not just to distance you from Hashem—it's to steal your energy.

And it explains why sometimes a person feels inexplicably drained, cloudy, or spiritually numb after doing something wrong. It's not psychological guilt—it's spiritual loss.

Teshuvah: The Spiritual Reset Button

The good news—and it is revolutionary—is that teshuvah rewires everything.

Rav Addes brings the Arizal that teshuvah is not

just regret. It is a spiritual process that:

- Cuts off the power supply to impure forces,
- Cleanses the blocked channels of the soul,
- Restores the alignment between your actions and your source.

And when it is done with sincerity, it can even cause previous spiritual losses to reverse. In the language of Chazal:

"Great is teshuvah, for it transforms sins into merits."

That means the spiritual system doesn't just heal—it evolves. Your soul grows more sensitive. Your intuition becomes stronger. Your connection to Hashem becomes clearer.

And with that, the gates to the supernatural reopen.

Learning Torah with Intention: The Most Powerful Technology on Earth

In one passage, Rav Addes explains that even a person who is tired, distracted, or unlearned, but who opens a sefer and **tries to learn Torah with desire,** can awaken spiritual lights so powerful that angels cannot describe them. He writes that even if you don't understand everything, the very effort itself generates **rivers of spiritual influence.**

He warns, however, that these lights are often subtle at first. The soul may begin to sense things before the mind catches up. A deepening of insight. A softening of emotion. An inexplicable desire for truth. These are not coincidences.

These are signs that your **system is activating**.

The more you learn, the more you align. The more you align, the more you receive. And the more you receive, the more you can transform the world around you.

What This Means Practically

- Your soul is a real, structured system directly rooted in the Divine.

- Torah learning is not symbolic—it is a spiritual mechanism that creates energy, clarity, and power.

- Mitzvot are tools for activating and expanding the soul.

- Sin blocks that energy and gives power away—but teshuvah restores it.

- With consistent Torah study and spiritual integrity, a Jew becomes a conduit for supernatural influence.

This is not an abstract idea. It is a **living system**, and it's open to anyone who's willing to begin.

Bitachon
The Hidden Switch That Unlocks Everything

The Final Gate is Not Intelligence. It's Bitachon

At this point, you've seen that the soul is real. You've seen that Torah learning and mitzvah observance channel Divine energy into the self and the world. You've seen how sin blocks the system, and teshuvah clears it.

But none of it will activate **none of it will flow** without one essential key:

Bitachon. In English, we call it "trust in Hashem." But that phrase doesn't capture the full truth. Bitachon is not just belief. It is not just optimism. Bitachon is a **state of spiritual posture** a deep inner certainty that:

"Hashem is running everything, and He is good. I am safe with Him. I can move forward, because He is holding me."

Without that posture, a person may do all the right things and still feel spiritually dry. With it—even the smallest action can ignite a fire.

Bitachon: Not Optional, But Foundational

In the sefer Pirkei Machshava, Rav Addes writes that bitachon is not a comfort for hard times; it is the **engine** of the entire spiritual system. He compares it to the connection between a device and its power source. A device may be sophisticated. It may be beautifully constructed. But without the plug in the wall, **it remains off**.

Bitachon is the plug.

It is what connects your soul to its Source in an active way. It transforms "knowing about Hashem" into living with Hashem. And that transition is the core of all supernatural power in Torah.

Because supernatural power does not mean "magic." It means transcending the limits of nature through closeness to the One who created nature.

And only bitachon opens that door.

Bitachon Is More Powerful Than You Think

Many people misunderstand bitachon. They think it means passively "hoping for the best" or pretending to be calm. But in Torah thought, bitachon is an **active force**.

It is the belief that:
- Hashem can change anything in a moment.
- Hashem desires your good more than you do.
- Your success does not come from your intelligence, skill, or effort—it comes directly from His will.

This trust **opens the spiritual channels** that allow blessing, healing, insight, and Divine help to flow. Not because bitachon is magical—but because it aligns the soul with reality.

And reality is: Hashem is in control.

Rav Addes explains that bitachon changes a person's spiritual "gravity." Just as physical gravity draws physical objects downward, **bitachon draws spiritual energy downward**. It pulls yeshuot (salvations), refuot (healing), and giluy (revelation) into the life of the one who trusts.

Bitachon Unlocks Spiritual Flow in Real Time

When a person learns Torah but thinks, "This won't really change anything," the effect is blocked. But when a person opens a sefer and says to himself:

"I may not understand everything. But I know that my soul is eternal, and every word I learn matters. Hashem sees it. Hashem is with me. This matters more than anything else I could be doing right now."

That thought **changes everything**. It opens the soul. It clears the noise. It draws light down immediately—even if you don't feel it yet.

Bitachon is like flipping on the main power switch in a hidden control room. Everything begins to move.

Even the Struggle Itself Activates Power

One of the most beautiful teachings Rav Addes shares is that **even the desire to connect to Hashem,** even the struggle itself, sends waves of energy upward. He writes that when someone wants to do better but fails and still keeps trying Hashem counts it as success.

Why?

Because in the world of truth, intention matters.

Bitachon doesn't mean you think everything will go smoothly. It means you know Hashem is with you even when it doesn't seem like it.

In fact, some of the greatest spiritual power is activated in the moments you feel weakest, but still choose to learn, to pray, and try again.

Bitachon Changes;

How You Learn, How You Live, and Who You Are

With bitachon, learning Torah is no longer a task. It is a reunion.

With bitachon, mitzvot are no longer obligations. They are tools of transcendence.

With bitachon, even failure becomes holy. Even silence becomes prayer.

And this shift—the internal realignment toward complete trust—is what begins to unlock the hidden spiritual capabilities inside you. Insight. Sensitivity. Spiritual intuition. Deepened tefillah. Strength against the yetzer hara. Sometimes even things that seem outwardly miraculous.

Because Hashem supports those who trust Him—not as a reward, but as a law of spiritual design.

Bitachon Is Built Slowly

but It Builds Everything

If you feel far from bitachon, start small.
Tell yourself daily: "Hashem is with me. He wants me to come close."

Before you open a sefer, say: "This Torah comes directly from Hashem, and He's guiding me in it."

When facing a challenge, whisper: "I don't need to control this. Hashem is leading it."

This is not naïve. It is real. It will shift how your soul receives, how your heart responds, and how your mind works. You will become more whole. And in that wholeness, the supernatural becomes natural.

The Secret Has Always Been Bitachon

The early tzaddikim didn't access spiritual power because they had superhuman IQs. They accessed it **because they trusted Hashem** completely and lived knowing that He is the only true force in the world.

You can too.

You don't need to be a tzaddik to begin.

You don't need to understand every word of Zohar, every halacha, or all of kabbalah.

You only need to say, from the heart:

"Hashem, I trust You. I want to live with You. Teach me, guide me, hold me. I will do my best."

That's the best start.

From that moment, the system begins to awaken. From that moment, the gates begin to open.

And what begins as trust becomes something greater:

Supernatural closeness. Supernatural strength. Supernatural life.

Who we are and what we do

"Yeshivas Hamekubalim Nefesh Hachaim" merits being located in Yerushalayim on Har Tzion adjacent to Kever David Hamelech. The yeshiva is a pioneer in publishing siddurim and machzorim with the Kavanot of the Ariza"l specially geared to the beginner. Our siddurim are printed in an unabridged, clear format. They include instructions, introductions, and various customs written in a clear and easy style specified for our day and age. They also feature various prayers, intentions, charts and expanded Roshei Teivos to assist those wishing to enter these gates of wisdom. All this is done with nice fonts and typesettings which facilitate easy reading. Many of those who got used to our siddurim claim they cannot substitute it for any other kind.

Throughout the years we've expanded the repertoire of seforim we publish to incorporate a few types of siddurim, machzorim, tikun chatzot and books on various subjects. We also plan on publishing B'ezrat Hashem, a Tehilim, seforim on halachot and customs, commentaries on the Ariza"l writing and other Kabbalah seforim, Siddurim for women, Seder for Hoshana Raba night, shavuos night, Shvi'i Shel Pesach, books on segulos and personal prayers, a book of songs for Shabbos and festivals, Seder for Chanukas Habayit, Seder for a Brit Yitzchak, and prayers for the illui nashama of the niftarim.
"Yeshivas Hamekubalim Nefesh Hachaim" merits encouragement from gedolei Torah of our generation

and is especially endorsed by Rabbi Yitzchak Goldstein Shlit"a Rosh Yeshiva of Diaspora Yeshiva.

We are presently occupied with publishing our siddur -"Siddur Chen" with english introductions explinations and instructions. Many years of painstaking work was put into it so far. It is a result of much effort of our group that gathers to study the introductions and Kavanot of the Ariza"l. The siddur incorporates introductions, charts and explanations to ease the understanding of these Kavanot. We are simultaneously working on Ashkenaz, Sefard, and Safardi siddurim, in three languages, Hebrew, English and Spanish.

Is it permitted to translate and why?

Many ask if is it permitted to translate Kabbalah literature into other languages. There are multiple answers to this question. The main response is that the unfortunate situation today is that there are some charlatans out there, many of whom aren't even Jewish, that present themselves as Mekubalim. Unfortunately , many Jews fall prey to them. Therefore anyone with the power to protest has the obligation to do so. He should also publicize as much as possible the correct way to approach these gates of wisdom. He should educate the masses that there is no way to fulfill their desire of attaining this wisdom other than the authentic Jewish way that was passed down for generations. If anyone tries to attain this wisdom elsewhere he will destroy rather than rectify. Therefore, we feel it to be not only permitted but important to translate these seforim of Kabbalah to make our people aware of the aforementioned.

Another reason to translate these seforim is that many

observant people throughout the world feel distant from spirituality. All their Torah and prayer are done by rote and just to fulfill their basic obligation to feel free to be able to move onto matters they find more interesting. We are confident that if they would taste the sweetness of the wisdom of Kabbalah, or even just some insights into what they are already doing, they would quickly be transformed to serious Ovdei Hashem. As they begin to see and understand how the whole Torah is connected to, and effects the higher worlds, they will get a new realization of what Torah is, and a renewed spirit.

Sharing the merit with you

It goes without saying that these projects are costly. Production is not progressing as quickly as it should fitting such a worthy project. We therefore extend our offer to all of Am Yisroel to participate in this tremendously holy project. Please take a generous part in funding the continuation of these important works. These are works of rishonim who are compared to angels. Through helping produce these works one can arouse the zchusim of the Rabbis who brought this profound wisdom down to us. This will also be the cause of elevation to their souls, and in this merit they will pray for us all to receive limitless bounty and blessing, Amen.

What else is in it for you

The Chofetz Chaim wrote in his sefer Ahavas Chesed that there are people who want to do something special in memory of a loved one. Sometimes they make a nice expensive tombstone with golden letters and nice flowers. Some add nice plants and the like and spend a fortune on these items. They think this will cause some pleasure to their departed relative. They are gravely mistaken. If heaven forbid a relative passes on and didn't leave any progeny behind, instead of investing in the above items, they should make an everlasting memory for them with a mitzvah that will endure for generations. If he doesn't have the means for this he should at least donate a Sefer in his memory, for the public to learn from, and write the name of the departed inside. This way whenever someone learns from it it will cause pleasure to the nifter. The Chofetz Chaim concludes that he's seen many do this.

This merit is multiplied many times over if one would dedicate the publishing of a new Siddur like the one we are working on. This would help many Yidden throughout the world pray to God with the proper kavana and to draw down to the world a spiritual and physical flow of blessings in all areas. This would also bring the geula closer. How meritorious would these sponsors be in this world and the next! They will be among the mezakei harabim that regarding them is written "They are like the stars forever", for this is a merit that lasts forever.